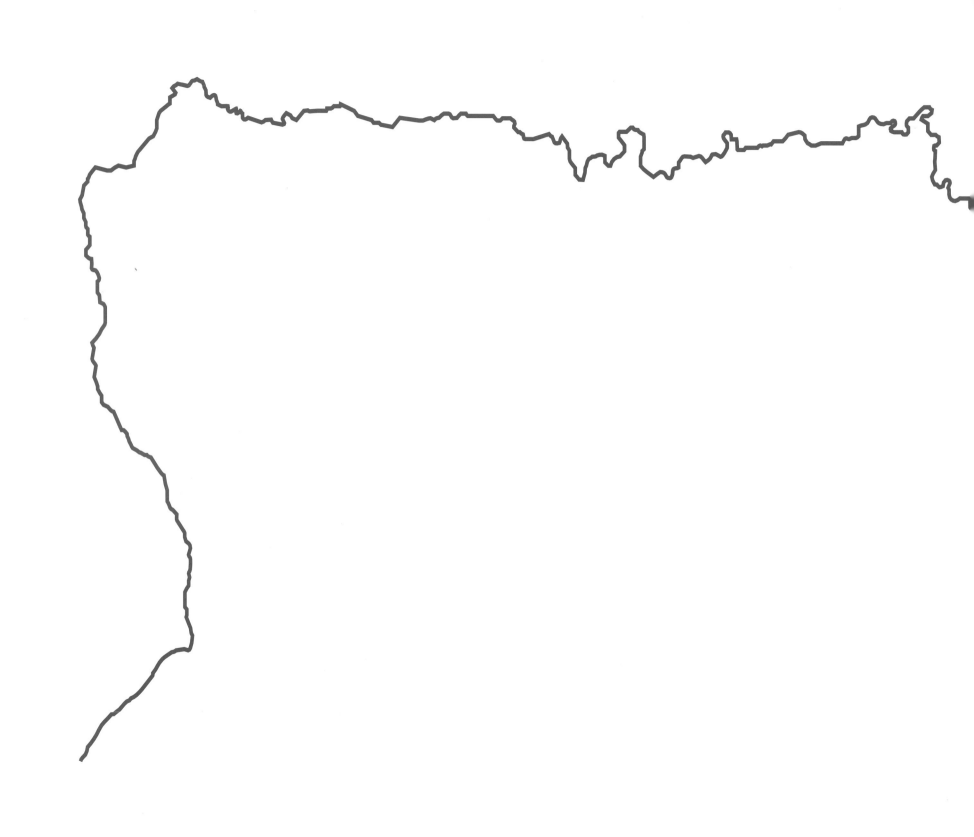

Riverwalk

Explorations Along the Cache la Poudre River

Riverwalk

Explorations Along the Cache la Poudre River

photographs by William Wylie
with a foreword by Merrill Gilfillan

UNIVERSITY PRESS OF COLORADO

Copyright © 2000 by the University Press of Colorado
International Standard Book Number 0-87081-583-0

Published by the University Press of Colorado
5589 Arapahoe Avenue, Suite 206C
Boulder, Colorado 80303

Printed in Hong Kong by C & C Offset Printing Co., Ltd.

The University Press of Colorado is a cooperative publishing enterprise supported, in part, by
Adams State College, Colorado State University, Fort Lewis College, Mesa State College,
Metropolitan State College of Denver, University of Colorado, University of Northern
Colorado, University of Southern Colorado, and Western State College of Colorado.

The paper used in this publication meets the minimum requirements of the American
National Standard for Information Sciences—
Permanence of Paper for Printed Library Materials. ANSI Z39.48-1984

Library of Congress Cataloging-in-Publication Data

Wylie, William, 1957–
    Riverwalk : explorations along the Cache la Poudre River / photographs by William
Wylie ; with a foreword by Merrill Gilfillan.
        p. cm.
    ISBN 0-87081-583-0 (alk. paper)
    1. Cache la Poudre River (Colo.)—Pictorial works. 2. Larimer County (Colo.)—Pictorial
works. 3. Weld County (Colo.)—Pictorial works. I. Title.

F782.L2 W95 2000
917.88'68—dc21
                                                    00-044722

09 08 07 06 05 04 03 02 01 00   10 9 8 7 6 5 4 3 2 1

to Kay

. . . our native country is less an expanse of territory than a substance; it's a rock or a soil or an aridity or a water or a light.

—GASTON BACHELARD, *L'Eau et les Reves*

Foreword
by Merrill Gilfillan

There is a place on the upper Cache la Poudre River that is difficult to leave. A place both lovely and out of the wind, where the river swings to the north edge of the valley and cuts itself a comfortable way there, leaving a broad meadow where on a good fall day the aspen in their little choirs know they couldn't find a better point to quake and flame. A relenting place after the pinch and press of the canyon gorges, where kinglets sing and the scent of willow and alder warms and drifts in the sun. And the river itself — the river with perhaps the most ear-catching name in the central Rockies, challenged only by the Medicine Bow — runs at its most provocative prime. A place one could sit for days, or weeks.

As a free river, the last of the undammed rivers on the Colorado Front Range, the Poudre's course is elegant and sure-footed for most of its hundred miles from Rocky Mountain National Park to its juncture with the South Platte east of the town of Greeley. Naturally the knowledge that it is an unimpeded flow (a free river is to an impounded stream as a goldeneye is to a barnyard fowl) lends music to it all, a sort of Bach keyboard accompaniment, but as an entity the Poudre is inherently both wild and poised, with a sangfroid worthy of its last-of-a-kind cachet.

The Cache la Poudre's classic life cycle, from sassy brook to dozing elder, illustrates the laws of river physics as clearly as any stream I can call to mind. Compared to rivers like the Plattes, it has a manageable scale both conceptually and physically. In half a day one can travel its entire course, stopping to consult at its various stages and ages, to test its various tones.

That place some thirty miles up the canyon, for example (they call it Indian Meadows), its blending of mountain and dale, of sage-brush harsh and Juneberry lush, reactivates without fail that most primal of conceits: river as creature, as willful thinking thing.

The Cache la Poudre was so named in the early nineteenth century by trappers who stowed a load of gunpowder in a pit on the river's bank. What the Arapahos called it I have never learned; but some of the lofty mountains in its upper drainage they named the White Owls, and perhaps they called the Poudre that. White Owl. Snow Owl. Ghost Owl. In any case, they recognized it as an estimable area, that gifted valley where it slips out from the mountains. It's reported that they requested, futilely, land along the middle Poudre for their reservation when the time for such things came. (The wide handsome flats across from Vern's Trailer Park and gas station near LaPorte would make a perfect sundance grounds.)

Moving water, whether mountain rapids or lazy Kansas stream, incites both reflection and play. It is a good wager that in the human universe rivers exist (beyond the cool splash in the face and the watering of the corn) to remind the species of the long-standing but easily forgotten verities of Motion-within-Stillness and Stillness-within-Motion; of the unified weave of the Eternal and the Always New. As such they are catalytic assets to whatever culture gathers on their banks. The English writer H. E. Bates noted that in regions of his acquaintance, rivers and the human populace along them acquired similar traits, moods, mentalities. The citizenry along the Nene, like the river flowing by, were drab and even mean; while inhabitants along the Ouse were as soft-spoken and gentle as their river.

Most settlements in the Rocky Mountain west are far too young to display any such deep symbiosis with their streams, and human generations have become so compulsively mobile that it seems unlikely to occur in this interglacial era. But, given a river, there are always relations. Boys dawdle along the banks, lost in far-side-of-the-moon adolescent thought. Fishers fish — the Poudre is prime water, off-course nymphs and spinners dangle in its trees. And there are signs of more tangential relations. In Greeley, traces of a weathered, maybe Kennedy-vintage treehouse droop in a craggy willow hanging out above the right bank. Out at the Poudre's junction with the South Platte, spent shotgun shells left by dove hunters are scattered in the grass. Along the riverpath at Fort Collins an empty Jack Daniels bottle rests under the Russian olives. A Rottweiler still wet from a dip sits near its reading mistress, hungrily watching a pair of mallards float by.

Where the Poudre emerges from the canyon just above LaPorte into the swaled hills and tilted last-of-the-ouzels uplifts, it takes on a mentality that is one of both Grand Entrance and vulnerability. From Fort Collins on east, however, the Poudre is a more contemplative presence. The Poudre of the plains is less glamorous to most eyes, but it carries an unhurried pensiveness of its own. And when you want to know what it's thinking, you find a sizable cottonwood, or, with luck, a grove of them, and sit down there, cock your ears and consult. Cottonwoods are the *fruits* of western rivers, especially on the plains where they are dominant; they speak for their streams and embody their life-giving strength. A flow without them, like the upper Niobrara or the buzz-cut middle Arkansas, is a whimpering thing. (There is a white barn and farmstead on the Poudre just below Picnic Rock with a formidable grove of huge leaning specimens; I am always tempted to drive back the long lane and knock at the door to ask, "May I look at your cottonwoods?")

A full-scale grove of those trees is a wonder of makeshift and secret gregarious power. Gangly and elephantine, humble, myopic, massive. Flouting all conventional notions of symmetry and form, so utterly off in their cottonwood world, it's as if they continually gaze off into the sky in the hopes that no one will notice them, that they might be left alone to live their unassuming century. Most mature cottonwood groves are comprised of a single generation of trees of roughly the same size, a fact explained by the infant trees' need for full sunlight; they cannot compete in a shaded understory. When a grove dies of old age at 50, 75, 100 years, it is replaced by a complete new cohort — siblings, if you like.

It gives the groves a familial, herd-like appearance, and a feeling of stately measure, of headlong yet bemused purpose and plan. Even a single matriarchal tree of good girth conveys that heavy, clear-eyed sense of ancient thick-skinned witness, the mute testimony one finds most often in buttes and mountains, that sensation of panorama well-anchored. But a full-blown grove is like the chorus in the old Greek plays — wise, wizened, barnacled as whales, full of deep savannah calm.

So you note them along the Poudre, as along other prairie rivers, file them away in your mind and watch for them the next time down that road, admire them as you pass. Or, given the chance, stop when the weather is right, walk out and sit down there with a Bosc pear or a book of Walt Whitman, and consult.

〜

And there is a place on the lower Poudre — a handsome, unsuspected place Bill Wylie showed me some time ago — that garners the full essence of the river. It is a rarity on the plains Poudre: a place with ample elbow room and the native grasses in situ, where rough hulking hills rise sharply from the valley with a boldness and untouched quality reminiscent of the wild upper Missouri River in Montana. Most all the lower Poudre valley is crowded territory by my standards, heavily speckled with farms and silos, and even this place is wedged (ironically, I suppose, but who can tell anymore?) between a sprawling Kodak plant on the far shore and a county park celebrating a retired Atlas missile silo on the hilltop above. But it is a durable relic area most certainly and can serve even as the heart of the entire Poudre drainage.

These hills, bluffs almost, have the deep-rooted cushion of grama and buffalo grass, yucca and the sages, and, down in one of the skunkbrush-lined gullies, that odd high plains, suddenly-out-of-the-wind stillness. Prairie dogs yap from an upper table; a freight train blows to the north. Scattered car tires, rusty oil drums, an old bedspring lie here and there on the slopes. A pair of whitetails jumps from one of the miniature canyons, bounds off among the little sandstone hoodoo formations.

From a promontory the Poudre is visible below, swinging, sidestepping, breaking into a brief flurry of whitewater where it rams the cliffs, then reconsiders. Through binoculars I follow its course to the east, downstream toward Greeley, where I remember the Poudre as a harassed thing, penned and hammered by quarries and polluted almost into unconsciousness, rolling and drifting like a keelless wounded creature.

I stroll down into the bottomland and walk over to the river, placid enough right here, good, complex company. A half-dozen battered veteran cottonwood stand on the bank, an attenuated would-be grove. And downriver a quarter mile there is a fine one, a three-masted loner of graceful design. Its remnant frost-brittled leaves pitter and patter in the late October breeze like raindrops on an ordinary tree. It must be close to seven feet through at eye-level.

Then I climb back up, following a four-wheeler track through the ruddy little bluestem, and find a windless nook to sit in. Front and center on the western skyline the snow-capped mountains where the Poudre begins shimmer in the sun. It is a good interior exercise to envision, while looking up at those peaks, the distinguished and just-so dash of a sandbar that lies where the Poudre enters the South Platte. This is the perfect place for bird's eye upstream/downstream thoughts. I even find myself recalling "L'Allegro" and "Il Penseroso" for the first time in a good many years.

The more I think of those mountains as the "White Owls" the more I like the name. It would be another worthy exercise to visit these hills with snow on the ground and to visualize the Poudre coming all the way through a snow-owl landscape. What one finally glimpses after consciously courting a river is the sense of the entire course as a unified organism; as a lengthy Common. Remembering that rivers are the oldest moving things, and despite the western American water laws, the Poudre is a Common. All she wants to do is reach the South Platte.

But a Common, especially a hundred-mile Common, can be difficult to grasp in any sensible, sensuous way, bird's-eye-view or not. In fact the only way to know it is to walk every foot of it as Bill Wylie has done. And the fact that he brings back pictures from the Poudre is an added beneficence and testimony. The old Roman orators around the time of Cicero held among their persuasive arsenal a strategy they called *topographia,* the skillful evocation of a place as part of a convincing oration. Bill Wylie's photographs, with their wide-ranging eye, carry that sort of evocation-by-extended-detail, that kind of stirring evidence that someone is out there looking, noticing, valuing a facet of this Aesop world. They argue for the endlessly various textures of the Poudre, the marginal glints and hidden crannies, the joy of flotsam. And above all the countless formations of light, light playing on the basic elements of earth and air and water — each visual intersection "One day and one day only."

These photographs from the Poudre and its edges are here to remind us of all that is fragile and possibly salvational in the river: water taking on the look of obsidian; the genius of cottonwood bark; the astral whorl of eddy froth; wind over sandpiper tracks. To salute and remind us of the long, thin Common and the muscle of its flow.

These photographs were made over a period of four years at various locations along the Cache la Poudre River. From its source as snowmelt on the Continental Divide to its confluence with the Platte on the eastern plains, the Poudre is in effect a "working" river. Overutilized by agriculture and recreation, threatened by the possibility of a dam, the waterway is the focus of much attention and debate along the Front Range of Colorado. Although many sites retain the marks of human occurrences, the river itself remains wild and full of possibility.

In his book *Science and Human Values* Jacob Bronowski states, "We come to know a thing only by mapping and joining our experiences of its aspects." By paying attention to landscape we can begin to think about our place in nature; pictures allow us the quiet necessity of close inspection. — *WW*

4

6

12

14

15

16

20

25

30

38

42

Acknowledgments

I would like to thank Kerstin and Robert Adams, Ellen Allman, Angela Brayham, Doug Dertinger, Jan and Richard DeVore, Corey Drieth, Gary Huibregtse, Edith and Emmet Gowin, Eric Ming, Karen Murray, Eric Paddock, Chris Pichler, Adam Schreiber, and David Woody for their encouragement and support. Eric Elshtain walked and fished most of the river with me. I am grateful for his friendship. Scott Lindsten carefully and patiently worked on the original design and layout. I am forever indebted to Merrill Gilfillan for the elegant essay that begins this book and honored by the friendship we have established. Laura Furney, Darrin Pratt, and the staff at University Press of Colorado patiently helped me through the process of preparing the book for publication. The Colorado Council on the Arts provided crucial support during the development period of the project, and the Stryker Short Foundation provided support for the book's production.

    Most of all I want to thank Kay Jenkins. Her enthusiasm, commitment, and love are a big part of every aspect of this book and, more importantly, my life.

About the Photographs

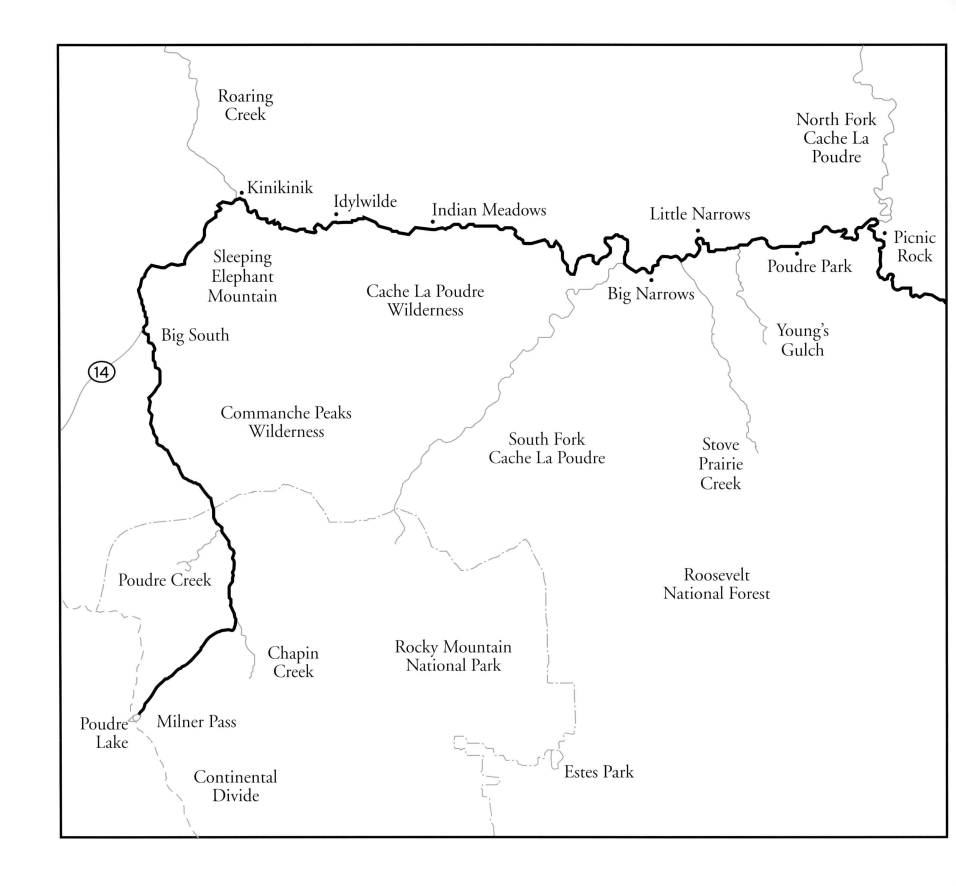

Roaring
Creek

North Fork
Cache La
Poudre

Kinikinik

Idylwilde

Indian Meadows

Little Narrows

Picnic
Rock

Sleeping
Elephant
Mountain

Cache La Poudre
Wilderness

Big Narrows

Poudre Park

Big South

Young's
Gulch

14

Commanche Peaks
Wilderness

South Fork
Cache La Poudre

Stove
Prairie
Creek

Roosevelt
National Forest

Poudre Creek

Chapin
Creek

Rocky Mountain
National Park

Poudre
Lake

Milner Pass

Continental
Divide

Estes Park

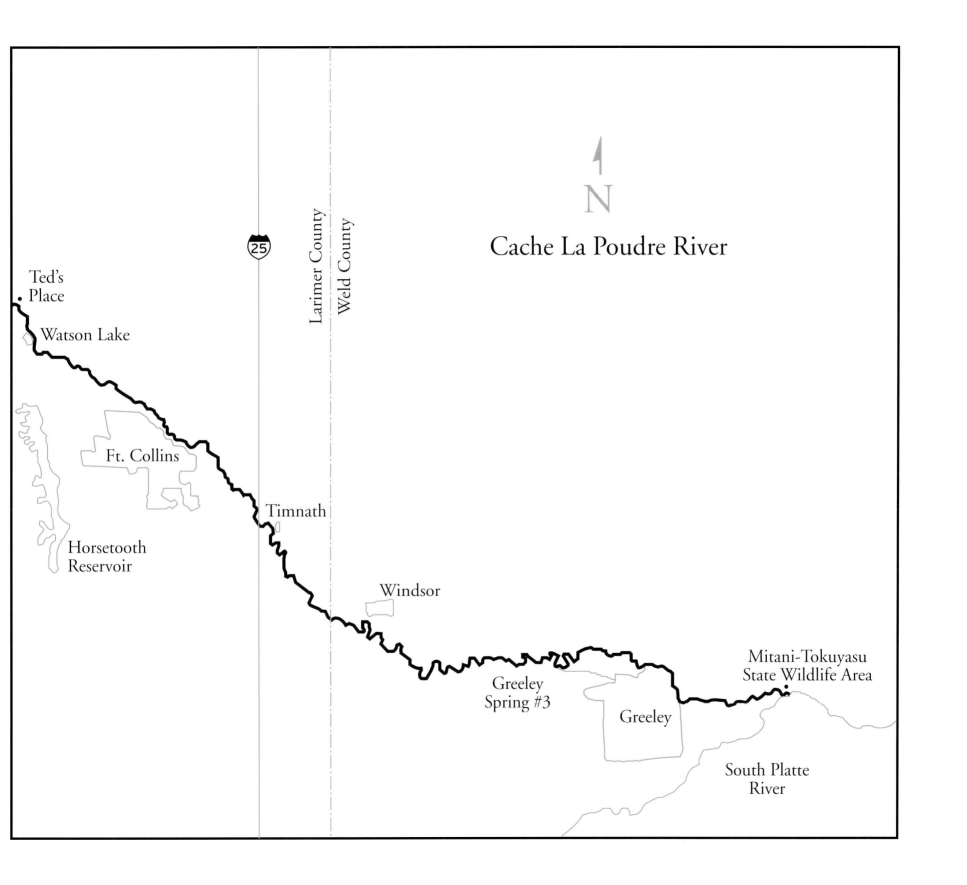

Cache La Poudre River

N

Ted's Place

Watson Lake

Larimer County

Weld County

25

Ft. Collins

Horsetooth Reservoir

Timnath

Windsor

Greeley Spring #3

Greeley

Mitani-Tokuyasu State Wildlife Area

South Platte River

WILLIAM WYLIE was born in Harvey, Illinois, in 1957 and moved to Colorado in 1976. He received an MFA in photography from the University of Michigan in 1989. After eighteen years on the Front Range of the Rockies, he currently resides in Charlottesville, Virginia, and teaches at the University of Virginia. His photographs have been widely exhibited and can be found in numerous public collections, including The Art Museum at Princeton University, Amon Carter Museum, and the Denver Art Museum. In 1998, he received an Artist Fellowship from the Colorado Council on the Arts.

MERRILL GILFILLAN was born in 1945 in Mt. Gilead, Ohio. He attended the University of Michigan, where his poems were awarded a Major Hopwood Prize, and the University of Iowa Writer's Workshop (MFA, 1969). He is the author of Magpie Rising: Sketches from the Great Plains, which won the PEN/Martha Albrand Award for nonfiction, Sworn Before Cranes, a collection of short stories that won the Ohio Book Award, Burnt House to Paw Paw: Appalachian Notes, and, most recently, Chokecherry Places: Essays from the High Plains, which won the Western States Arts Federation 1999 Award for Nonfiction and the Colorado Book Award.